WATER UNDER GROUND

Isaac Nadeau

The Rosen Publishing Group's
PowerKids Press™

New York

To Anthony, Nathan, and Erica

Published in 2003 by The Rosen Publishing Group, Inc.
29 East 21st Street, New York, NY 10010

First Edition

Editor: Gillian Houghton
Book Design: Maria E. Melendez

Illustration Credits: Cover and title page, landscape, all border designs © Photodisc; all illustrations created by Maria E. Melendez.

Nadeau, Isaac.
  Water under ground / Isaac Nadeau.
    p. cm. — (The Water cycle)
Includes bibliographical references and index.
  Summary: Provides information about what happens to water under ground and what effect that water has on the Earth.
  ISBN 0-8239-6263-6 (lib. bdg.)
  1. Groundwater—Juvenile literature. [1. Groundwater. 2. Water.] I. Title. II. Series: Nadeau, Isaac. Water cycle.
GB1003.8 .N34 2003
551.49—dc21

2001005147

Manufactured in the United States of America

CONTENTS

river

ocean

lake

glacier

UP, DOWN, AND UNDER GROUND

Water is always on the move. The frozen water of a glacier moves very slowly. The rushing water of a waterfall rushes off a cliff. Under ground, water flows in caves and through the soil. As it moves from place to place, water can change shape. Water can be a solid, a liquid, and a gas all in the same day.

Wherever it goes and whatever form it takes, Earth's water is always part of the water cycle. The water cycle is the movement of water throughout Earth. Clouds, rain, rivers, lakes, glaciers, and oceans are all part of the water cycle. Water beneath Earth's surface plays an important role in the water cycle. Most of the time, underground water is hidden from view, but it is always in motion. Eventually all water makes its way to the surface.

◀ *From high in the sky to deep under ground, water is on the move almost everywhere on Earth.*

Gravity pulls water from the atmosphere to Earth's surface in many forms, such as rain, snow, and hail. Some of this water **evaporates** quickly and returns to the air. Some runs downhill over the ground to join a stream, a lake, or an ocean. Some water is **absorbed** into the soil. This process is called **infiltration**. Water under ground might stay close to the surface, or it might sink miles (km) below it. It might be absorbed by the roots of plants and help them to grow. Groundwater might get very hot and boil to the surface. It might stay underground for only a few seconds or for many thousands of years.

Most of the world's water is in the oceans. A small percentage is frozen in glaciers and in polar ice. A tiny amount of the water on Earth is found in the atmosphere or in rivers, in streams, and in lakes. The rest of Earth's water supply is underground.

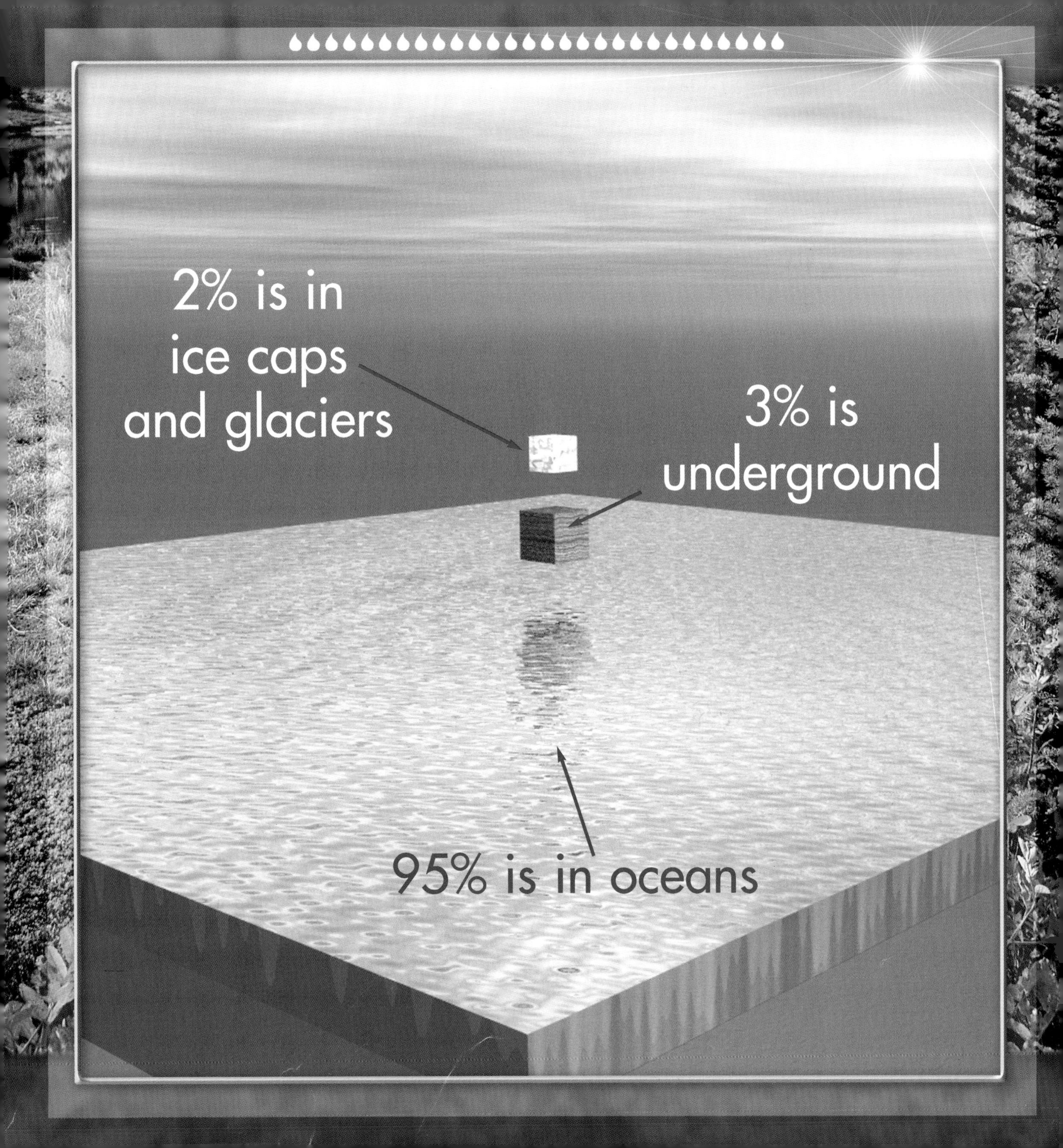
2% is in
ice caps
and glaciers
3% is
underground
95% is in oceans

unsaturated
rock

saturated
rock

WATER IN THE SOIL

The layer of Earth closest to the surface is called the soil. Soil is made up of many **particles** of different shapes and sizes. These particles have pores, or spaces, between them. As water falls to Earth's surface, gravity pulls it down through the soil. Through infiltration, the soil's pores begin to fill with water. All the living things in the soil, such as plants and insects, depend on this water to process food and to grow.

Beneath the soil are layers of rock. Some rock is porous. Porous rocks contain many tiny spaces into which water can soak. Ground that holds very little water in its pores is described as **unsaturated**. When water sinks to a place where all the spaces are already filled with water, the ground is described as **saturated**.

Soil varies by the types of rocks, plants, and animals in it and by how much water it holds. The ground is described as unsaturated (top inset) or saturated (bottom inset) depending on how much water it holds.

All the water in saturated ground is called groundwater. The water table is the uppermost boundary of this saturated zone, or area. The water table rises and falls depending on the amount of **precipitation** an area receives. After a heavy rainfall, the water table rises as the saturation zone increases. During a **drought**, the water table drops as the amount of water under ground decreases.

Recharge is the process of water flowing into the saturated zone and becoming groundwater. Any layers of soil or rock that are porous enough to store water and **permeable** enough for water to flow through them create an **aquifer**. An aquifer is an underground layer of porous rock that contains water. Many people get their drinking water by drilling wells into aquifers.

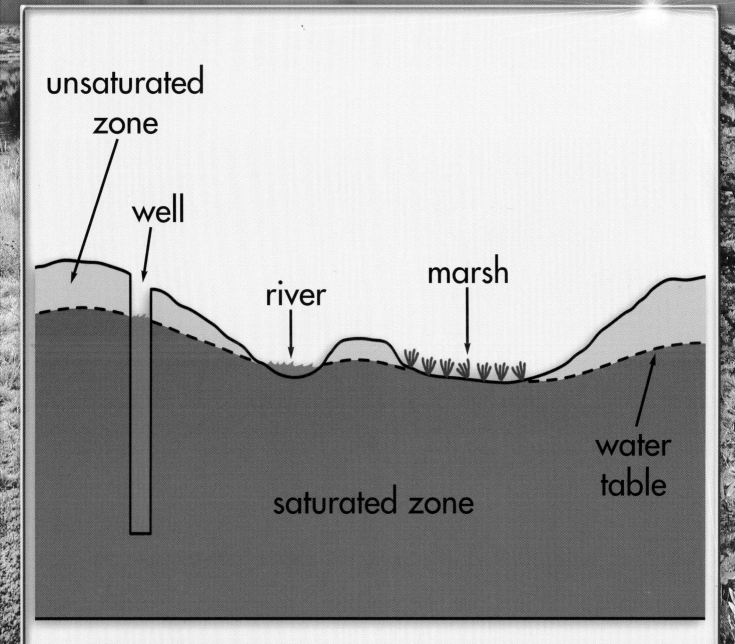

unsaturated zone

well

river

marsh

water table

saturated zone

The aquifer extends from the surface of the soil to the bedrock, or the layer of rock through which water cannot pass, beneath the saturated zone. Rivers and marshes form where the water table rises above the surface of the soil. Wells are often dug to tap the aquifer.

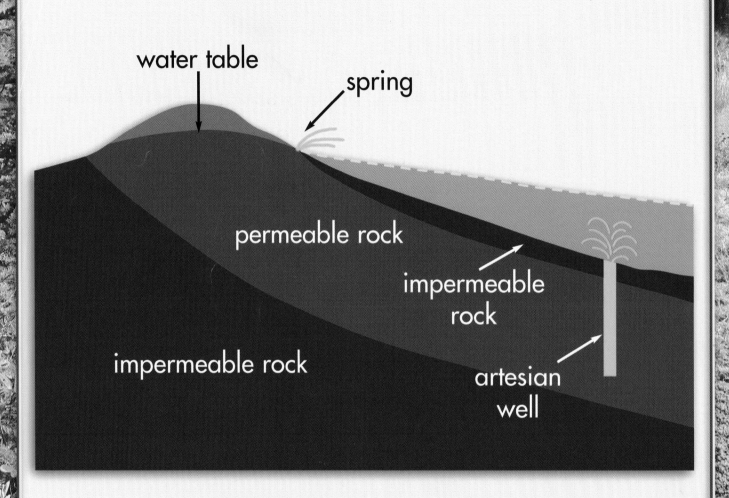

water table

spring

permeable rock

impermeable
rock

impermeable rock

artesian
well

A layer of permeable rock lies between two layers of impermeable rock. The groundwater in the permeable layer is under great pressure. Where the water table reaches the surface of the soil, water flows from the ground in the form of a spring. Where the imaginary line of the water table rises above the impermeable surface rock, artesian wells can be dug. Through artesian wells, water flows freely from the ground without a pump.

WELLS

People have been digging wells for thousands of years to bring groundwater to the surface. Where the water table is close to the surface and a shallow well reaches the saturated zone, wells can be dug using picks or shovels. Today most wells are made using drills. Pumps, powered by machine or by hand, bring the water to the surface.

Often a well is dug or drilled into an aquifer trapped between two layers of **impermeable** rock. This water is under pressure. The water flows out of these wells without a pump. These wells are called **artesian wells**. Sometimes underground water flows naturally from an aquifer to the surface without a well or a pump. These places are called **springs**. Springs occur where the water table is at Earth's surface. Many streams are fed by groundwater springs.

HOT SPRINGS AND GEYSERS

Deep below the surface of Earth, the ground is heated by the planet's core, or center. In some places under ground, the rock is so hot that it melts. This molten, or melted, rock is called magma. Sometimes magma rises to Earth's surface and produces volcanoes. Sometimes magma stops just below Earth's surface, creating a hot spot under ground. The hot spot heats the surrounding groundwater to as high as 400°F (204°C). This superheated water rises toward Earth's surface until it finds an opening. Some of this water bubbles gently out of Earth in the form of hot springs. When the opening is too small or the pressure of the spring is too great, the boiling water and the steam are forced out in an eruption. This eruption of steam, called a **geyser**, repeats itself again and again. Some geysers erupt many times a day. Others erupt only once every few years. Many factors contribute to how often a geyser erupts. These include how much water is in the geyser, how hot the water is, and the size of the crack in Earth's surface.

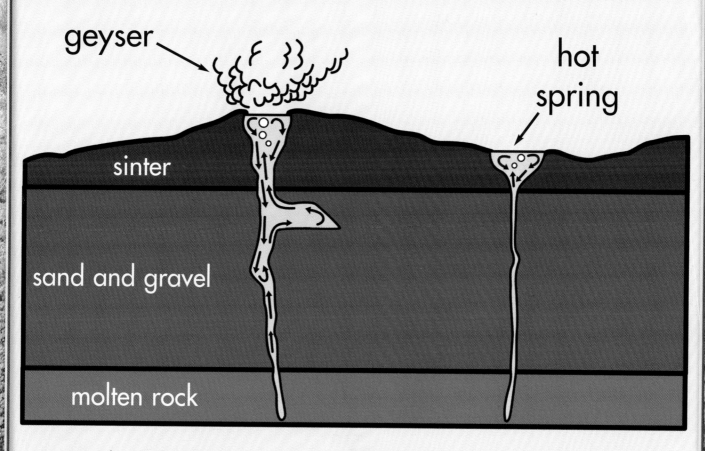

geyser

hot spring

sinter

sand and gravel

molten rock

Geyser tubes extend deep into the ground like the roots of a plant. Superheated water rises up the tubes toward openings in the sinter, a layer of rocks and minerals left behind by the steam and water of an erupting geyser. Geysers can erupt only a few inches (cm) high or can spray steam more than 150 feet (46 m) into the air. Steamboat Geyser in Yellowstone National Park has shot steam 300 feet (91 m) into the air!

soda straws

stalactite

column

flowstone

stalagmite

quartz crystals

The largest cave room in the United States is in Carlsbad Caverns in New Mexico. This underground room is more than 1,000 feet (305 m) wide and has a ceiling 200 feet (61 m) high. Caves can be decorated with a variety of natural formations, such as columns of rock and sheets of flowstone.

HOW CAVES ARE FORMED

*I*magine standing in a dark room the size of a movie theater. The only sound comes from water dripping on the stone floor. Now imagine that you are hundreds of feet (m) under ground, and that there is a chill in the air. It might be hard to believe, but the cave you are standing in was carved by water.

When rainwater falls through the atmosphere and soaks through the soil, it bonds with a gas called carbon dioxide. This gas helps water **dissolve** certain types of rock, such as **limestone**, as it flows through the pores in the rock. Water flows along existing cracks in the rock. As the rock dissolves, the cracks and the pores grow wider, allowing more water to flow into them. In time many of the spaces become tunnels big enough for people to explore. These underground rooms are called caverns, or caves.

Deep under ground, water carves out caverns and builds columns of rock called **dripstone**. Limestone is dissolved and carried away by water as the water saturates a layer of rock. This water travels through the pores of the rock and drips through the cracks and pores in the ceiling of a cave. As the water drips, some of the limestone clings to the ceiling, forming a hollow ring, called a soda straw, around the pore or the crack. With each drop, more limestone is added. The shape that is created, called a **stalactite**, looks like a hollow icicle made of stone. When each drop of water hits a cave floor and evaporates, more limestone is **deposited**. This rock grows upward toward the cave's ceiling. This formation is called a **stalagmite**. Stalactites and stalagmites can grow together to form a column of rock.

soda straw

stalactite

column

stalagmite

As water drips through the pores in the ceiling of a cave, limestone is deposited, forming a tube called a soda straw. Through time, many layers of deposits form enormous rock decorations. A large dripstone column can take 100,000 years to form!

Some water is so deep under ground that the deepest wells can't reach it. This water might remain underground for thousands, or even millions, of years before making its way to the surface. Other sources of underground water reach the surface every day. Yellowstone National Park (above) is home to thousands of small surface vents, such as geysers, hot springs, paint pots, and fumaroles, which release water and steam into the air.

UP, UP, AND AWAY!

All groundwater eventually makes its way back to the surface. Groundwater that comes back to the surface is called discharge. Water comes to the surface through wells, springs, or geysers. It also comes to the surface when the water in an aquifer reaches a riverbed. The water joins the water in the river on its way to the ocean. Many rivers and lakes would dry up if groundwater stopped flowing into them.

When it makes its way back to the surface, groundwater is not groundwater anymore. It becomes part of a river, an ocean, or a spring. It becomes water in the roots of plants. It evaporates and becomes tiny drops of water in a cloud. Eventually the water will return to the ground and become groundwater again.

*I*n some places, people pump groundwater out of aquifers faster than it can be recharged. People in these areas must learn to protect the supply of clean water. They must try to use only what they need, so that there will always be clean groundwater. The amount of water on Earth will always be about the same. Water is constantly being recycled and reused. However, the amount of clean water that is available depends on how people use it.

Water can become polluted by the chemicals used on farms and in factories and mines. This polluted water can soak underground into the groundwater. As more people depend on groundwater, we are learning how important it is to make sure the water stays clean. Clean groundwater is important for plants, fish, and all living things.

GLOSSARY

absorbed (uhb-ZORBD) Taken in and held onto by something.

aquifer (A-kwuh-fur) A layer of sand, gravel, or porous stone that holds water.

artesian wells (ar-TEE-zhun WEHLZ) Wells drilled into aquifers whose water is under pressure.

deposited (dih-PAH-zuht-ed) Left behind.

dissolve (dih-ZAHLV) To break down.

dripstone (DRIHP-stohn) Cave formations made by water and limestone.

drought (DROWT) A long period of dry weather with little or no rain.

evaporates (ih-VA-puh-rayts) When a liquid becomes a gas.

geyser (GY-zer) An eruption of hot water and steam from a crack in Earth's surface.

gravity (GRA-vih-tee) The force that causes objects to move toward the center of Earth.

impermeable (ihm-PUR-mee-uh-buhl) Not allowing water or other substances to pass through.

infiltration (in-fil-TRAY-shun) Water soaking into the ground.

limestone (LYM-stohn) A rock that is easily dissolved in water.

particles (PAR-tih-kuhlz) Tiny pieces of something.

permeable (PER-mee-uh-buhl) Allowing water or other substances to pass through.

precipitation (preh-sih-pih-TAY-shun) Rain, snow, or any moisture that falls from the sky.

saturated (SA-chuh-rayt-ed) Completely filled with water.

springs (SPRINGZ) Where groundwater flows out at Earth's surface.

stalactite (stuh-LAK-tyt) A stone formation that hangs from the roof of a cave.

stalagmite (stuh-LAG-myt) A stone formation that grows up from the floor of a cave.

unsaturated (uhn-SA-chuh-rayt-ed) Not completely filled with water.

23

INDEX

WEB SITES

To learn more about water under ground, check out these Web sites:

http://ga.water.usgs.gov/edu/mearthgw.html
http://water.usgs.gov/outreach/poster4/Poster4.html
www.usgs.gov/education/learnweb/caves/intro.htm